True H
of
The Driskill Hotel

By

Monica L. Ballard

Copyright © 2013 Monica Ballard
All rights reserved.

ISBN-13: 978-1932226874

Foreword

Of the thousands who have crossed the threshold of this Austin landmark to rest, to dine, to drink, to celebrate or to gawk, there are some who have remained behind, extending their "stay." Collected by the guides of Austin Ghost Tours, and compiled by tour guide Monica L. Ballard, these are the true stories of the staff, guests and ghosts of Austin's most haunted building, The Driskill Hotel.

Acknowledgements

The author wishes to thank Jeanine Plumer, Elizabeth Garzone, Nathan Jerkins, Alexander Hamilton (the tour guide, not the President), John Maverick, Cecily Johnson, Genevieve Johnson, Byron King, our tour guests, the staff and management of The Driskill Hotel and the more "spirited residents" of the hotel who led us in unique ways so that their stories may be told.

*Cover photography by Jen Reel,
courtesy of Texas Observer.*

Cover title & book design by Robin Kressbach.

Author's photo by Cecily Johnson.

Table of Contents

Chapter 1 — Austin's Most Haunted Address 1

Chapter 2 — So, How Many Ghosts ARE There? 3

Chapter 3 — The Three Most Common Forms
   of a Haunting 5
   1. Movement of Objects 5
   2. An Out-of-Place Aroma 8
   3. Dimensional Shift 11

Chapter 4 — Haunted Rooms and Hallways 17
   Phantom Staff 17
   The Little Girl in the Hall 18
   The Vortex on the 4th Floor 22

Chapter 5 — The Senator's Daughter 27

Chapter 6 — Other Driskill Ghosts: 34
   The Known Entities 34
   The Empress in the Mirrors 34
   Mrs. Bridges 39
   The Watchman, Peter Lawless 40

Chapter 7 — The Unnamed, Unknown Entities 44
   The Grey Ghost 44
   The Texas Ladies Man 45
   Annie Lennox's Wardrobe Consultant 47
   Animal Spirits 48
   The Playful & Helpful Spirits 49

In Closing… For Now 53

Chapter One
Austin's Most Haunted Address

There is a lot going on at the intersection of Sixth Street & Brazos. Some of the activity you can see; some you cannot. I'm not referring to paranormal activity, as such. You see, under the streets flow ancient artesian wells. In turn, these springs bubbling to the surface have watered related businesses throughout Austin's history. 6th & Brazos was once the address of the city's bathhouse. Just up Brazos at 7th Street stood Madame Templeton's "Miracle Eye Water," a headquarters that mailed vials of healing, mineral-rich water to destinations around the world; waters which, according to various testimonials, resulted in astounding cures. One block south, a modern bar owner excitedly showed me the basement of his establishment with its cistern intact. I could still hear the trickle of that underground wellspring whispering beneath.

So it was here where the bathhouse stood, that cattle baron Col. Jesse Driskill decided to construct his hotel by tearing down the previous ramshackle business and installing plumbing over the artesian. The new construction employed limestone, marble, cast iron pillars, glass, and brass. Combine these ingredients with the movement of those underground springs, and the materials act as conductors of electricity and energy in general. Add to that the continuous, and seemingly non-stop civic celebrations: everything from gubernatorial inaugural balls and weddings, to nightly happy hours, and this dynamic, bivalent power pumps, beating like a happy, healthy heart, attracting and holding not just energy but spirit energy. In paranormal circles, this is known as the "stone tape theory." I ran this hypothesis past a group of geologists on a private tour, and they deemed it to be entirely feasible. It could be what makes the Driskill Hotel, to quote a popular film, "Spook Central."

Chapter Two
So, How Many Ghosts ARE There?

In January 2010, Austin Ghost Tours' founder and manager Jeanine Plumer and I were on a flight to Hollywood to be featured on the premiere episode of the Biography Channel's program My Ghost Story because of a photograph that a tour guest took in the Driskill lobby.

"You realize that one of the questions they're probably going to ask us is how many ghosts haunt The Driskill Hotel," I warned her.

So we began reviewing all of the stories we knew and which spirit we could attach to that story. When we got to 19, we stopped. We agreed, if asked, we would just tell the producers, "a bunch of ghosts."

We have since come to terms with the impossibility of saying exactly how many spirits haunt The Driskill. It would be like asking someone at the front desk how many people are in the building at that moment. While they might be able to estimate staff and registered guests, that number is greatly augmented by patrons in the bar and restaurants, as well as tourists wandering in and out. As in the living world, so it is in spirit world. Some ghosts find release, while other, new spirits take their place because of the "battery" nature of the building. We can only review the evidence of our own encounters and listen to other people's experiences, documenting as we go, and finding commonalities in the stories.

Chapter Three
The Three Most Common Forms of a Haunting

In order to tell many of the ghost stories of The Driskill, it is necessary to understand the various ways spirits make themselves known.

1. Movement of Objects

One of the ways ghosts manifest themselves is through the movement of objects. This includes interfering with plumbing and electricity, both seemingly easy for spirits to manipulate.

When one of the rooms on the 5th floor of the historic portion of The Driskill was the scene of a young woman's suicide in the 1950s, not many guests could get a good night sleep in there. The room was transformed into an office area, then a maintenance area, then storage. The management at the time eventually walled off the doorway leading to the bathroom. At the commencement of the 21st century, the hotel management had changed. When they heard that this room wasn't being used because of its history of ghostly occupation, they sniffed skeptically, "Ghosts? Why, that's a room we could be renting out!"

So they asked the maintenance staff to break through the walled up doorway as the first part of renovations. When they did so, they found the inaccessible bathtub on the other side filled with clean, clear, freshly drawn water.

There is a regular guest of The Driskill who has become great friends with Austin Ghost Tours' staff. She visits from California, so let's call her "Cali." Cali always books a certain room on the 5th Floor, not because of the view or amenities, but because she is fond of the painting to the left of the door. One of housekeepers told Cali of a mischievous ghost who would often turn the light back on after the room is readied for guests and the door is shut.

"I hear it click and reopen the door to find the light back on," the housekeeper confides. "I'll turn it out, but when I shut the door, I'll hear the light switch click again. I unlock the door, and the light is on again. This happens several times until I give up and decide to leave the light on!"

Cali told us that she made an agreement with the mysterious occupant of that room that she is okay with items being moved, provided they were not relocated in front of her. This agreement was proposed after the following experience:

> *"I was putting on make-up in the bathroom and went to reach for my tube of cover-stick and it wasn't there. I thought I had taken it out and left the silver tube lying on the black countertop. I wondered if I had walked around with it and left it*

the other room for some reason. It wasn't in there. Fortunately, I had a spare with me, so I dug that out of my make-up bag and applied it. When I went to put it back in my bag, the original silver tube was back, standing upright directly in front of me on the black counter."

Once Cali offered this agreement with the ghost not to float anything in front of her, the spirit still found an interesting way to say hello. Cali came into her room one night to find the soap reoriented perpendicularly to the length of the soap dish. "Very funny," she murmured to the "empty" bathroom, and after washing up, she laid the soap horizontally, as it should be. When she got up the next morning, the soap was standing on end in the dish. Well... at least it didn't move it in front of her!

Oddly, I ran into a Canadian couple after a tour one evening with a similar story. The previous evening, once they had settled in for the night, the wife was looking forward to enjoying a bath in the huge Roman tub, but she could not find the plug for the drain even though they both saw it sitting on the side of the tub when they first checked in. They ended up stuffing a washcloth into the drain instead. The following morning when the husband went to take his shower, the plug was back—perched on the side of the tub where they could not have possibly missed it—and no one but the two of them had been in the room since then.

We're often asked, "What does a ghost want when it acts that way?" and Jeanine will shrug and respond, "Sometimes they just want to let you know they're around."

2. An Out-of-Place Aroma

The scent of cigar smoke often wafts through the halls of this non-smoking hotel, and an out-of-place aroma represents the second most common form of a haunting. Usually phantom aromas appear quite suddenly, and, just as abruptly, vanish. These aromas are usually tobacco or floral scented, or reminiscent of decay. And while the aroma of cigar smoke is often attributed to Col. Jesse Driskill, is the smell really caused by the ghost of the hotel's namesake? We have little way of ascertaining the truth.

Legend has it that in the mere five months that he owned The Driskill from December 1886 through May 1887, the Colonel could often be seen glad-handing guests in the lobby and dining rooms, puffing on a cigar. On the other hand, once he sold the hotel to his brother–in-law "Doc" Day, (no, he did NOT lose the deed in a high-stakes poker game, as rumored by many), Jesse Driskill did not visit at the hotel very often after that. Financially broken by the loss of his cattle in the Spring Freeze of 1888, Col. Driskill suffered a stroke in 1890, passed away, and was buried in Austin's Oakwood Cemetery in the family plot. Did those few years as a hotel owner seize enough of his spirit for it to take up residence in the building bearing his name?

When The Driskill opened for business, a tobacconist shop did occupy the lobby. William Sydney Porter, a budding author who later took the pen name O. Henry, worked there as a clerk. Might our cigar-smoking phantom just as likely be the owner of that shop, a customer, or some well-heeled frequent guest? Admittedly, it is just an easier leap for many to attribute the aroma of cigars to the bigger-than-life gentleman whose portrait hangs prominently in the lobby.

A security guard once followed Austin Ghost Tours guide, Nathan, as he led his group. When Nathan concluded his stories, he asked the guard if he had anything to add. The guard spoke of when he had first joined the staff and was teamed up with another guard for training. One day, however, the "newbie" reported in to find that his more seasoned partner had suddenly quit! He phoned his erstwhile co-worker to ask what was up, and the former guard said that he was making his rounds through the old stairwells where you can still see the original brickwork of the historic building. He smelled tobacco smoke and leaned over the rail, expecting to see a guest trying to sneak a smoke. There was no one there. Suddenly, a deep male voice over his shoulder asked, "Got a match?" He turned swiftly to find only empty air – and he quit on the spot.

Was it Col. Driskill himself? Possibly. There was an instance when a full-bodied apparition resembling him was seen smoking in one of the rooms. A tour guest on one of our Pub Crawls shared this story with me.

A gentleman who often comes to Austin on consulting trips prefers to stay on the mezzanine level. He had the

LBJ Suite overlooking, you guessed it, Austin's most haunted intersection, 6th & Brazos. In the dead of night, the consultant awoke to see a man smoking a cigar standing by the window. Pulling the drapes open, the intruder stared out at the sparse traffic. The consultant called out as he fumbled for the lamp switch next to him, "Hey, fella, what the hell are you doing in my room?" The tall gent said nothing but looked in the guest's direction disdainfully, as though to reply, "Your room?" When the consultant snapped on the light, ready to face his trespasser, there was nothing left of the specter except a lingering cloud of cigar smoke and the drapes still gently swaying from having been opened.

Cigar smoke isn't the only scent indicative of a spirit presence in The Driskill. Some believe that a former member of the housekeeping staff from circa 1900, a Mrs. Bridges, still remains fussing around the lobby, mezzanine and bar areas, rearranging flowers at tables long-since moved. Someone who worked for a floral company that provides arrangements for weddings and special events once told me that they were proudly taking pictures of their arrangements on the mezzanine floor before the event started. It wasn't until later, looking at the photos, that they saw the faded image of a woman in an old-fashioned uniform adjusting some of the stalks of flowers.

Tour guides and guests alike have picked up on the aroma of roses. Each time we've encountered this mysterious floral scent, we've looked around to see if there were real arrangements nearby that could account for the odor. Tour guide Alex was in the lobby one evening when he had his own experience:

> "My allergies were bad that night and my sinuses were completely stopped up. But suddenly, the scent of roses was overpowering! I was meandering around the tour guests to see if someone was wearing perfume, trying to be as subtle about it as I could! I knew that an out-of-place aroma was indicative of a haunting, but didn't know about Mrs. Bridges and the rose scent until I mentioned this odd experience to another tour guide, Elizabeth."

One evening as my Pub Crawl guests were relaxing on either side of center aisle of the bar, one of them sat up at the exact time I did. We caught one other's eyes, and the guest exclaimed, "Something just went rushing by us! It smelled like… roses!" I responded, "Mrs. Bridges is in a hurry!"

3. Dimensional Shift

The third most common form of a haunting can be described in several different ways. When you feel as though you're being watched, when the hairs on the back of your neck or your arms stand up, when the air around you grows chill or you sense a static charge, all are indications that something extraordinary is about to happen or is taking place at that moment. Personally, I needed a name for this phenomenon, so I started calling it "Dimensional Shift."

I experienced two instances of Dimensional Shift at The Driskill on the same morning in February of 2009. Barry, the cameraman from *My Ghost Story* and his assistant were meeting Jeanine and me to capture some interior shots for when our segment was going to air. Dressed in my customary Victorian costume, I arrived early for the shoot and was sipping tea in the lobby when I felt it. Static in the air around me increased. A tingling sensation crawled over my scalp, and I looked up and around. The only activity in the lobby was a gentleman descending the grand staircase and continuing into the lobby. He did a double take as he spotted me. I patted my name badge and called to him reassuringly, "No, I'm real. See?" He choked back a worried chuckle and retreated for the sofas near the Brazos entrance.

When Barry, his camera assistant and Jeanine arrived and we began the shoot, this same businessman approached us and hesitantly asked, "Are you talking about ghosts? Do you mind if I tell you about experiences I had last night and this morning?" The businessman then paraded us to the mezzanine level to the Cattle Baron Suite, one of the finest in the hotel.

"First of all, when the bellman led me into the suite, the room reeked of cigar smoke," he told us. "But the next time I came in, it was as though it was never there!" Jeanine and I shared a knowing glance. The Cattle Baron Suite was rumored to have been one of the Colonel's favorites.

Leading us to the room where he slept, the businessman

paused at the door to the second bedroom with two double beds. "I thought about sleeping in there, but I got a kind of weird feeling, so I slept in the one with the king-size bed instead." Now the glances included Barry and his assistant, neither of whom were strangers to haunted locales. The glance said, "Oh, we are SO checking out the weird bedroom at some point!"

Earlier in the pre-dawn darkness, the businessman got up to use the bathroom and while crawling back into bed, took a quick look at the bedside clock to check the time when something pulled the bed curtain a good four or five inches to block his view of the clock. We tested to see if movement on the bed could cause that to happen, but the bed curtain was too far away from the mattress. Then the businessman said something very interesting: "It was as though someone read my mind and said, 'Oh, you want to see what time it is? Nope! Not gonna let you!"

On the way to his private dining room where he had another story, I suggested that we take a look inside the other bedroom that creeped him out. I was the first to step over the threshold, and as I did, I felt the electrical field around my body warp as though someone had thrown a charged net around me. It felt as though I had stepped through a force field. I blurted out, "Oh, my God!" in astonishment at the weird sensation, and Jeanine coaxed me back out through the door into the hall. She readied her freshly battered camera and took one step into that room, only to have the batteries drain immediately. As all of us cautiously entered, the static charge in the air was palpable.

Whatever was in there with us, however, seemed to flee, perhaps not as curious about us as we were about him or her!

From there, we went into the businessman's dining room and Jeanine took the seat across from him. "That's where my lead sales guy was sitting when it happened," he forewarned. "He and I were going over what we got accomplished here in Austin, what we were going to follow up on when we got back to San Diego, that sort of thing. Suddenly, he got the weirdest expression on his face. It seemed to be a combination of astonishment, fear and amazement. He leaned across the table and hesitantly whispered, 'Right… behind you!"

Behind our businessman was a tray of beverages on a credenza. Part of the collection of drinks was one bottle with a paper flyer that read, "Republic of Tea." The salesman nervously reported that something pulled the flyer to the opposite side of the bottle as though to read it… and then pushed it back to its original position. The businessman had enough. He told his salesman, "That does it! The rest of this meeting happens downstairs in the lobby. I'll see you down there in five minutes."

I should note that this is when the gentleman came downstairs and I experienced that Dimensional Shift sensation, as though the particles of his experience rippled out, signaled and interacted with my energy field—so much so that it attracted my attention!

Does spirit activity reach out to us in the manner most likely to be received? Is this why different people simultaneously perceive the same haunting in varying ways? Or are multiple messages trained in our direction every day with only the strongest signals able to make it through the barrage of interference we know as everyday life? Would I have been "alerted" to this man's descent into the lobby if I had been talking or texting?

I believe that the ability to perceive Dimensional Shift comes with tuning out the noise of the living. This can come with conscious effort through meditation techniques or it can happen naturally when one is relaxing or engages in some mindless task. This is why many of the Driskill ghost stories we hear from staff and guests start out, "I was dusting on the 4th floor...," "I was setting up for a reception in the Maximilian Room...," "I was shampooing the carpets...," "I was reading in bed...," "I was watching TV and getting ready to call it a night." Could brainwaves lowering from noisy Beta to the more relaxed daydream state of Alpha diminish the veil between dimensions?

Another reason for activity to spark in any of the 3 Forms of a Haunting is the spirit version of the "cocktail party effect." We have found that by recounting the history of the place or people during a tour or investigation, responses occur and activity increases. A few things could be happening here: it is possible that discussing the events of a place or person "keys in" on a familiar frequency that attracts something or someone on another dimensional level. Perhaps what is taking place is that the thought particles of the person speaking as well as those hearing and imagining what might have taken place in these rooms, hallways and ballrooms activate some sort of energy that is perceived as light or sound anomalies. Hauntings that are not interactive or "intelligent" but rather "residual" may attract our attention due to commonalities in external conditions: weather, humidity, noise level, or brainwaves. In other words, there may be more scientific opportunities to explain hauntings than we fully understand at this time.

Chapter Four
Haunted Rooms and Hallways

Of all the stories we have collected from The Driskill staff, some of our favorites come from managers and security. These people, after all, are the skeptics who join the staff and are warned by others on the force, not just about the ghosts, but the would-be ghost hunters who wander the hotel in the wee hours in search of their own first-hand encounters. Security and management are there to make sure the guests remain undisturbed and that customers stay safe. But I don't know if dealing with the paranormal is included in the training manual. Usually the new employees are on staff for about three weeks when a select few, as one new manager put it, are "welcomed by the hotel."

Phantom Staff

One recent addition to the security staff shared his story with Jeanine of when he had first started. He was in the hotel late at night and approached a staff area that can only be accessed by a keypad. As he came down the hall, he thought, "I hope I remember my code correctly. The light is dim by that keypad." But when his hand reached for the pad, the lights on either side of the door brightened enough for him to put in his code and open the door. "That was odd," he thought to himself as he entered the employee-only area. On the other side of the door, he passed a young lady walking out and said, "How are you?" just to be courteous. "Fine. Have a good night," she responded before exiting. "Should I tell her about the door and how the lights brightened?" the new security man thought for a split second. "No, why would I tell her that?" And then it hit him. "Who was that?" and then more strongly, "Who was that?" He dashed back out the door and peered into the empty bar. No one. He leaned over the railing to the lobby and asked the front desk staff if they had seen anyone. No. "Here's what puzzles me more than anything else," he told Jeanine. "As part of security, I may forget your name, but I'm trained to remember faces. This woman's face is a total blank to me. All I remember was that she was wearing a long dress. That alone should have struck me as strange, but it didn't at the time. I was a total skeptic before that night," he confided. "Not anymore!"

The Little Girl in the Hall

I was astonished one night to hear a story from one of the toughest guys on the security staff. One evening, though, as I was savoring a glass of wine in the lobby after a tour, this same man – let's call him Bruno to protect his identity – sat beside me and we were pleasantly chatting. A tourist drawn to my costume and badge approached and asked, "Is it true this hotel is haunted?" Before I could answer, Bruno spoke up. "Oh, yes! I've had my own experience with the ghost of the little girl!" I sat back in my chair astonished. "This I've got to hear," I exclaimed, and Bruno did not disappoint.

"You know that painting on the 5th floor, right? The one of the little girl holding the letter and flowers?" Indeed I did! Numerous tales floated around that painting. One theory supposed that she was the infamous Senator's Daughter who in 1887 stumbled as she chased a ball down a flight of stairs, fell and broke her neck. While the ghost of the Senator's Daughter is often seen by children and a few adults, and experienced by others through touch, sounds and in other ways, we at Austin Ghost Tours are certain that the little girl in this painting is not the Senator's Daughter, despite the mythology. People often report that the little girl's eyes follow them as they pass and they get a sensation of dizziness when they stare at the painting. (Stare unblinking at anything for a few minutes and you're likely to feel dizzy.) Nonetheless, Bruno had heard of the experiences of other staff members regarding this painting, so perhaps he was influenced by those instances.

> *"That painting always gave me the heebie-jeebies, but my wife said, 'You need to go make peace with that little girl. Tell her you're there to protect her.' Well, I felt foolish as all get-out, but one night as I was making my rounds, I went to the painting, introduced myself and said just that. And then to seal the deal, I took her picture with my cell phone: one photo from the left, one from the right. I was about to take one from the front, but someone*

called me on my earpiece and said I was needed in another part of the hotel. So I left the 5th floor and never made it back there the rest of my shift. But when I got home, I told my wife that I did what she suggested, and asked her to download the photos from my phone to the computer while I took a nap. When I got up, she said, 'I got those three photos off your phone.' I said, 'You mean two photos.' She said, 'No, there were three.' I asked her to show me. And, sure enough, there were three pictures of the painting. One from the left, one from the right, and the one from, pardon the expression, dead-on. But I never took that third photo. And here's something really weird: there was this effect of an oval frame around her face – something my camera phone can't even do!"

A few months later as I was finishing up a busy Halloween night telling stories in The Driskill lobby, when a new manager, William, shared how he was "welcomed by the hotel." Some prospective guests asked to see a suite on the 5th floor right next to the infamous painting. As he led them there, he noticed the light bulb above the little girl's painting seemed to be burned out, so he radioed maintenance to come up and check on it. In trying to show the suite to the guests, the keycard refused to open the door. When the card was swiped, the lights indicated that the deadbolt was in place inside the room, but the room was vacant! William called for assistance and someone from security showed up. He had the same problem, but after a few tries, the door unlocked. While the guests were examining the room, the security man commented to William, "That was weird. It would have to be near her painting and on Halloween, no less. Did you notice her light is out?" William thought little of it, said that he had called maintenance, thanked security, and went inside the room to wait for the guests. When he exited a moment later ahead of the guests, the first thing he noticed was that the light over the little girl's painting was back on. The security man was at the other end of the hall, smiling. William whispered accusingly at him, "You messed with that light, didn't you?" The security man responded, "I swear, man, I passed by and said, 'Happy Halloween' to her and it came back on! I just wanted to see your face when you came out!"

Did that security man tamper with the light bulb? Probably not, considering what William told me next. That gentleman hadn't always worked as security. He had been part of The Driskill's In-Room Dining staff at one time. He was delivering a service of wine and glasses on a tray. When he passed the painting of the little girl, the glasses and wine bottle began whirling on the tray uncontrollably. When he stopped and collected himself a few steps later, he realized where he was: the little girl smiling innocently right beside him. It is unlikely that he would show her disrespect in any sense.

Bruno's experience and William's testimony are two of many stories about that painting, and I began to wonder, even though we know it isn't the Senator's Daughter, could she have "attached" herself to that delightful image? It would, after all, give herself a face she could show to many who might not be aware enough to sense her presence. The painting allows guests to come to her, rather than her always going somewhere to interact with them. Jeanine remains uncertain about that idea for now. But that's what keeps this business interesting. Theories and postulations may have to suffice until more convincing evidence can be examined.

Not all questions can be answered solely by evidence, however. In fact, sometimes the best evidence simply raises more questions. That was certainly the case when Haunted Texas and Austin Ghost Tours investigated one of the hotel's most haunted rooms.

The Vortex on the 4th Floor

In 1991, 23-year old Tara was looking forward to a spring wedding in Houston when her fiancé called off the event with just a few days to go. Distraught, she tried unsuccessfully to take her own life at the Houston Hilton her first night following the break-up. "Borrowing" her former fiancé's car, she drove to Austin and checked into The Driskill. Legend has it that on her second day in town, she went on a massive shopping spree, charging thousands of dollars on his credit cards. However, the police report testifies that she only made a few inexpensive purchases such as a carton of cheap beer, a People magazine and one other item. As rumors swirled through the years, she became a Houston "socialite" carrying armfuls of shopping bags, breezing back to the hotel. The real picture is much sadder.

After downing nine beers of a twelve-pack along with hard liquor, she examined the instructions for that one new item among her purchases: her brand new revolver. Loading it, she put the "Do Not Disturb" sign on the door and bolted it, grabbed a pillow from the bed, and facing herself in the bathroom mirror, shot herself in the stomach, the sound muffled by the pillow. The police report indicated that if the bullet had not killed her, the alcohol level in her bloodstream would have.

Eight years later, two female hotel guests saw the bride's full-body apparition late one night in the hallway of the 4th floor, which was closed for renovations. Considering that the concierge confirmed the identity of the lady whom the women had spotted, Tara's ghost must have been reported by others before that. In fact, many rumors abounded about strange activity around that room; so much so that when the renovations were completed in 1999, hotel managers changed the room numbers around to put a stop to the stories. But experiences continued to circulate even with the different room number and soon a cast of new spirits were seen, heard and experienced there.

The spirit of a maid from the 1940s has been encountered watching and sometimes interacting with guests. She even chided one guest about how to use the phone in that room! Some guests, uninformed of the haunted nature of the room, comment that they feel as though they're being watched. Occupants remark that the sound machine designed to play soothing wind chimes, surf or nature sounds will start blaring upon entering the room. While shooting a TV segment, I was describing the moments following Tara's fatal shot, when, suddenly, the bedside radio came on and the announcer began commenting on a classical piece he had just played based on the Song of Solomon: "Love is as strong as death," we heard him intone. It was an eerie moment that unnerved the cameraman and his assistant. When Jeanine, Nathan, and I held vigil in that room in 2006, we saw luminous orbs floating around us, felt a skittering across the bed, heard keys jangle and experienced someone knocking on the door, only to find no one there when we answered it.

In the summer of 2010, Austin Ghost Tours began hearing about phone calls to that room, but when guests answered the phone there would be no one on the other end. This story was becoming almost commonplace. Then later that summer, I had a speaking engagement in North Carolina, and I wanted to take the audio clip with me of the keys jangling and the phantom door knock. In transferring the audio from digital to analog format, I was astonished to find an additional male voice in the room just before Jeanine opened the door! (Nathan had left by then, so it wasn't him.) The voice said, "That was the call" and Jeanine was just as surprised to hear the recording as I was.

The meaning of "That was the call" mystified us until we heard yet another story about occupants in the room receiving a phantom phone call with no one on the other end. Then we had to ask ourselves: "Could the door knock with no one there have been "the call" for us? This raised further questions. Was the voice there all along, but we didn't "hear" it until we had the context of the phone calls? Or was the voice added to the recording once the phenomenon with the phone calls began?" Sometimes when you gather evidence like this, all you end up with are more questions.

A male voice, an African-American maid, manipulation of phones and electronics, knocking, multiple energies darting like slow-motion fireflies; it's obvious this isn't just the bride's room anymore. In fact, a Ft. Worth couple on my tour in September of 2010 shared that they were staying in that room and already their phone had rung three times with no one on the other end. Jeanine and I happened to be in The Driskill the following morning and, upon spotting the couple in the restaurant, I asked if any more unusual events took place when they returned after the tour. "Not last night," the woman reported, "but this morning as I stepped out of the shower into my locked bathroom, there was a message for me written in the steam on the mirror! It said, 'HEY!'" Jeanine and I were dumbfounded! "But that's not all," she continued, "Waaaay up in the corner of the mirror, there were two tiny shoe prints!"

"You mean hand prints," I suggested.

"No, shoe prints! Like a five or six year-old girl would wear!"

The Senator's Daughter, perhaps? The Driskill Hotel's original ghost from 1887? Ah, but that's another chapter.

Chapter Five
The Senator's Daughter

The first balmy Saturday afternoon of March 2010, I ventured downtown to take some photos and collect some new history and ghost stories from along Congress Avenue. I had recorded a dandy one from someone in the 900-block and was looking for a quiet spot to transcribe it while it was still fresh in my memory. I found myself in, of all places, the ladies room by The Driskill Bar. They have a comfy little settee in there, and it was deliciously quiet that early on a Saturday. But as I scribbled, I felt a little wave of dimensional shift wash over me. I started a new file on my digital recorder and asked aloud who was in the room with me. The whispered name came back, "Samantha." I was intrigued, but I left it at that, only sharing the recording with the inner circle of the tour guides and Dennis, the audio engineer for *Haunted Texas*, the TV series.

Fast forward to the night before Halloween, 2010. I had just finished a long night of storytelling in the Driskill lobby, greeting tour after tour. After a few minutes of "decompressing" (and enjoying the band at the annual Goodwill Ghoul Ball upstairs on the Mezzanine level,) I stood and turned to leave. It was then that I quite literally ran into Cali for the first time. She saw my name badge and commented that she kept meaning to take the tour the next time she was in town. A huge University of Texas fan, she usually visited whenever there was a Longhorn home game. "I always stay here at The Driskill," she told me. "The staff knows me ... I'm sure the ghosts know me ... Tara... Samantha –"

I stopped her abruptly. "Wait! Who is Samantha?"

She responded, "Samantha is the Senator's Daughter!" And then off-handedly added, "Well, that's what the staff calls her. I mean, they had to call her something!"

Had I waited another ten seconds to leave, or left ten seconds earlier, Cali and I might have never met. And I might never have learned that the staff had named their littlest ghost. I could not help but wonder how "accidental" our encounter was.

As mentioned before, legend has it that the Senator's Daughter accompanied her father to The Driskill Hotel when she met with her death. It was either for a special function of some kind or it was during the 1887 Legislative Session when the Texas Senate met at The Driskill since the most recent Texas State Capitol was still under construction. In either case, her father gave her a ball to occupy her as he tended to his politicking. The story goes that as she toddled off, unnoticed by her father, she lost control of the ball and it bounced down the Grand Staircase from the Mezzanine Level to the downstairs lobby. She took off after it, stumbled and tumbled down the stairs. Either she broke her neck and died there on the landing of the stairs or she was taken home unconscious and died there. You would think that because her father was in the Texas Senate that news of this accident would have been well publicized and easy to locate. Actually, just the opposite is true.

According to Austin Ghost Tours guide and genealogy buff, Elizabeth, the girl's young age would have prevented her from being mentioned in the census previous or after her death. Add to that the notoriety of her father and the fact that the hotel was in its first year of operation; these could very well hinder ever knowing the truth about this youngster's identity. Unless her death was written about in the Senator's family correspondence or a Driskill staff member's journal, it is unlikely we will ever discover who she or her family was. If this Senator was influential enough and Col. Driskill likewise agreeable, her unfortunate death might have been purposefully kept secret. Nonetheless, she is one of the more lively spirits romping through the hotel, even today.

I spoke with two hotel guests Morgana and Teana, who recently wandered the 4th floor of the historic portion of the building. They were walking down the hall when Morgana looked down to the carpet and took an extra step as though to avoid something. "I even felt as though I kicked something a little," she reported. Teana, hesitated too, asking, "What was that? It looked like a black ball of something!" When they looked around a moment later, there was nothing there. This strange phantom ball had disappeared.

As I led a tour group in through the Brazos Street entrance one Friday evening in early February 2010, the valet who opened the door gave me a wink. "Come back after your tour," he prodded. "I got a good one for ya!" He shared this story with me later that evening.

Some folks were in here last Saturday night. 20-somethings from Kansas, not guests, just having a few drinks at the bar. When the bar announced last call, they decided to hit one more place along Sixth Street to end their evening. Coming out of the bar, the first young lady in the group looked back at the others and said, 'Why is that child up at this time of night by herself? Where are her parents?' The others in the group looked in the direction of the Grand Staircase, then back at her and asked, 'What child?' She looked back toward the stairs, her face whitened and she murmured, 'We've gotta go. We've gotta go right now.' She made it out to our curb here, but then she had to sit down. Naturally, we gathered around and asked her friends if we should call the hotel physician. 'No,' they said. She had had maybe one too many, but mostly she was a little shaken up. You see, when they turned by the stairs to leave the hotel, she says she saw a little girl at the base of the staircase, wearing an old fashioned dress carrying a ball. The girl asked her to play. When her friends said they didn't see anyone there, she looked back. It was then that she noticed she could partially see through this child.

What made the valet's story so exciting for us at Austin Ghost Tours was that, up until then, most of the apparitions of this child were to other children. She would often appear to kids and ask them to play with her. Interactions with grown-ups were more commonly through touch or sound.

As I told this story to my tour group in the months that followed, I remember one particular night when a little girl broke away from her parents in the lobby and paused to listen, eyes shining with excitement. It was not until I invited my guests to take some photos and meet me by the door that I learned that this family was registered at the hotel. Some of my tour participants told me that when they were passing them on the Mezzanine floor, the young girl commented, "See, Mama? I told you a little girl asked me to play!" Then she pointed to another part of the palatial floor and exclaimed, "There she is with her ball!" But before she could break away again, my tour guests reported that her mother briskly yanked her through the open door and into the supposed safety of their suite. On two occasions (two years apart from each other) I have spoken with children who said a little ghost girl named Ruth asked them to play with her.

Every now and again, the Senator's Daughter reveals herself to an adult in an abrupt and unexpected way. There was the woman who was in the bar bathroom stall when suddenly she heard little footsteps dash through the restroom. She looked up to see a small child materialize through the door, look at her quite astonished, then take a step back through the locked door and disappear! Another woman was attending a reception on the Mezzanine when she felt a tugging on her long skirt. She looked down to see her skirt extended as though someone was holding onto it, and then it dropped. She heard a child's footsteps dart away. Instinctively, she told a staff member, "There's a child lost around here. She was tugging on my skirt!" But when the confused woman couldn't describe the youngster, the understanding staff member confided, "It's okay. We know who that is. She's fine."

Staff members at The Driskill have long reported that they hear a ball bouncing down the Grand Staircase, oftentimes when their vision is blocked by a large flower arrangement or such. They will hear a child's laugh and a ball bounce, and they'll stand off to the side by the banister, expecting to see someone, but nothing is ever there.

One of the earliest stories told to me about the Senator's Daughter concerned a woman who had just started working at the bar. It was after closing time and, although the staff does not generally use the public restrooms, her coworkers thought it would be okay for her to freshen up in the closest bathroom considering the lateness of the hour. She was in one of the compartment-like stalls, when she heard the main door to the restroom burst open, a little girl's giggling and footsteps across the floor. "Kind of late for a guest to be checking in with a youngster this time of night," she thought, "but I guess it's possible." When she exited and went to wash up, she looked around for evidence of this child. Just then there was bang on the door to her left, then the sound of a bounce and a catch. A pause, then the three sounds repeated. Bang! Bounce. Catch. Bang! Bounce. Catch. During the brief pause, the woman ran out and spilled out her story to the other bartenders. Rather than being horrified or even astounded, they simply smiled. "Congratulations," they told her. "You've met the Senator's Daughter!"

Think of it: when you wander these historic halls or the Mezzanine, take a stroll through the lobby or even visit the Ladies Room, you may never be more than a few steps away from The Driskill's youngest and very first ghost.

Chapter Six
Other Driskill Ghosts: The Known Entities

The Empress in the Mirrors

Legend has it that while Ferdinand Maximilian was traveling through Europe in the 1850s, he encountered a gypsy woman who stroked his palm, gazed into his eyes and predicted that one day he would be crowned as Emperor. Such a forecast appealed to Ferdinand and from that moment every contact he forged and every connection he strengthened was made with whispered hope of that prediction coming true.

He soon cozied up to French royalty who agreed that Ferdinand would indeed make an excellent figurehead for their puppet regime in Mexico. But he would need an Empress. Enter a distant cousin, Charlotte, Princess of Belgium and thoroughly willing to share the Maximilian name and Mexico's throne. They were married amid much pomp and set sail for the New World. Stepping ashore, "Charlotte" became "Carlotta", and the couple was welcomed by the dirt-poor peasants of Mexico on their way to Chapultepec Palace set on a hill on the outskirts of Mexico City.

Despite the gypsy's prediction coming to fruition, a fairytale ending was not in store for the Emperor and Empress. The French soon withdrew their support for this too distant empire because of the increasing threat of locally powerful Benito Juarez. Thinking she might have more sway with European aristocracy, Carlotta traveled overseas to solicit support for their teetering regime. The French court refused to see her. Ever resilient, she headed for Italy's aristocrats. Again, she was dismissed. She was awaiting an audience with the Pope when devastating news arrived: Juarez and his Mexican mercenaries had occupied the palace, overwhelmed Maximilian's forces, and executed Ferdinand before a firing squad. He gave his executioners an allotment of gold with the request that he not be shot in the face. They took the gold and ignored the request.

When word reached Carlotta, her heart broke and her mind snapped. She lived well into her 80s, being welcomed and sheltered by many European courts, always graciously received as "Empress Carlotta." Late in life, she spent many solitary hours with a doll as company, speaking to it tenderly and calling it "Max" until she finally passed and was led beyond the veil by her beloved.

Perhaps it was when she made this final transition that Carlotta learned of a belated wedding gift from Ferdinand that she never saw in life. Even as the couple separated, magnificent mirrors were on their way to Chapultepec Palace. Backed with diamond dust to add to their sheen and richly detailed, each mirror was crowned with a bust of Carlotta, Empress of Mexico. After Juarez's capture of the palace, the couple's furnishings were scattered and the mirrors ended up in San Antonio to be sold at auction. They were discovered in 1929 just in time for renovations at The Driskill. The men's smoking room on the Mezzanine was being transformed into a men's and ladies' dining room, and Carlotta's mirrors would make a perfect addition.

Since the gilded mirrors have graced the ballroom now dubbed the Maximilian Room, odd occurrences have been reported.

One of the earliest stories Austin Ghost Tours staff heard about the room took place during the 1990s when a photographer was setting up for a shoot of modern bridal gowns. He thought that the Maximilian Room's ornate appearance would offer a nice contrast to the modern gowns. As he was setting out cameras, lenses, and film at a table in the room's center, he heard the doors behind him open. He looked up and into the reflection of the mirror in front of him to see a stunning raven-haired beauty wearing a sumptuous antebellum white gown glide into the room. His first thought (after pausing to appreciate her loveliness and grace) was, "I thought we were going modern!" He turned to question this "bride" only to find that while the doors were open, there was no one in the doorway. He turned to face the opposite mirror. There she was, a vision in white, smiling at him. Whipping around to the doors – no one there! The next time he glanced into the mirror, she had disappeared. But he did a double-take when he looked more closely at the bust above the mirrors and noticed the remarkable resemblance.

The room is often set aside for wedding receptions that take over the entire Mezzanine floor; a fitting setting for the wedding cake, groom's cake, and coffee. It has also played host to meetings and luncheons. We often hear from the audio/video companies who, while setting up for the festivities, hear the swish of satin and see something in white flash past their peripheral vision. Thinking that the bride has entered, they'll look up to greet her only to find that there is no one there.

On more than a few occasions before a private tour when the hotel is quiet, I have wandered up to the Maximilian Room to chat with Carlotta. Once when I addressed the Empress and asked if she would give me an indication of her presence, the corner lamp – and only the corner lamp – turned off and then a moment later, on again. Excitedly, I led my group up there during the tour to share the experience, hoping for a repeat occurrence. Carlotta disappointed us. I had over-stepped propriety, perhaps, in expecting royalty to "perform" on cue.

Carlotta did redeem herself in my estimation in December of 2010 when I gave a private tour in honor of a young lady's 13th birthday. She treated her friends to Sunday afternoon high tea and a ghost tour. They were a jittery bunch, shrieking and nervously giggling with every story, despite my best attempts to assure them that The Driskill's ghosts are not a scary lot. Our final stop was the Maximilian Room, and when I shared the couple's tragic story, the girls were visibly moved. Lip trembling, one youngster asked, "Why would she haunt this room if she never saw the mirrors while she was alive? Wouldn't she rather be with Ferdinand?"

"It's my belief," I explained, "that when she got to the other side and learned the mirrors were a wedding gift from her husband, a strong connection was made with them at that point. I don't think she's trapped here at The Driskill, but I believe that when people admire the beauty of these mirrors, she's here to share that appreciation, like a hostess beaming and acknowledging her beloved."

To close the party, I suggested that we gather by the lovely Christmas tree for a group photo. And as we huddled together, I invited Her Majesty to join us in the photograph. As we waited for the snap of the camera, only the chandelier above the tree dimmed and illuminated again in response. These giggly girls, instead of shrieking in fright, at last breathed a quiet collective, "Wow!" Empress

Carlotta had made it clear: not all hauntings are about despair and darkness. Sometimes the reason for that spirit's visitation is love.

Mrs. Bridges

This paranormal staffer was a ghost I had heard about for many years, and I mentioned her before in connection to the smell of roses associated with her. She is another who has been known to appear to front desk staff, often when they are getting punchy in the wee hours. If things get a little rowdy, she manifests and "shushes" them, like a stern librarian.

In a manner of speaking, I feel as though I have seen Mrs. Bridges. I was allowing tour guests to capture some last-minute photos before continuing on. One woman noted a strange shape at the top of the grand staircase and I had her zoom in on it. There on the view screen of her camera was a woman in an old-fashioned long jumper and blouse, hair piled on top of her head standing on the top step both arms akimbo in surrender, her face in a frantic expression. "Wow!" I exclaimed, "I think you might have captured Mrs. Bridges! But I wonder what she's so upset about?" Just then, two Driskill maintenance workers carried an antique sofa down the stairs to another part of the hotel. It seemed clear to me that ghosts are like cats: they don't care much for change. Despite my imploring the guest to send us the photo, she was too "creeped out" by the woman's expression, and she deleted it. (Suddenly, I was the one with the horrified expression!)

The Watchman, Peter Lawless

Some of the earliest stories I had heard about ghosts at The Driskill included stories of a former ticket agent for the Great Northern Railroad, Peter Lawless. Mr. Lawless made the hotel his home after he became a widower, living on the 5th Floor for 31 years, even when the hotel was between owners. He had his own set of keys to the front door and his room. Each morning he would have walked from the hotel down Congress Avenue to the G.N.R.R. Depot, no doubt smiling when the trains arrived on time and grumbling when they were delayed. He attended Mass at St. Mary's Cathedral on Sundays, and had an active social life with civic clubs. Following his retirement, he was a known philanthropist to Seton Hospital, one of his favorite charities. But at least some of his spirit seems to have remained at The Driskill upon his passing, still marking time through old routines.

Those yarns I had heard and read from the 1990s and early 2000s described how the elevator doors by the front desk would open while early morning darkness still shrouded Austin. Mr. Lawless would step from the elevator, winding his watch, then nod to the front desk staff just before blinking out of sight. Other staff members had seen him on the 5th Floor as they were vacuuming or shampooing the carpet. Feeling the weight of someone's stare, they would turn off the machine and look down the hall to see a gent standing at the other end. Black hair, dark trousers, white shirt with old-fashioned collar, vest with a pocket watch on a chain, the specter would regard the employee for a moment, then turn and walk through a closed, locked door. I seem to recall another tale where he was spotted walking down the hallway in his bathrobe, an old-timey shaving cup and brush in his hand, still very much at home at The Driskill Hotel.

I had a tour guest who seemed somewhat unnerved by the Peter Lawless stories on the tour. She drew me aside at the close of the evening and confided, "You need to speak with someone at Cap Metro."

"The city bus service?" I wondered. "That Cap Metro?"

But lo and behold, we found someone who had an extraordinary experience early one morning. The driver was on her early morning route and rounded the corner of Brazos onto 6th. She suddenly braked and brought the bus to a halt, her dazed passengers startled by the jolt. They watched as she leaped off the bus, looked around and re-boarded, asking them, "What happened to that guy?"

"What guy?"

"That guy who jumped out in front of the bus just now! He was wearing a long vest and was holding one of those watches on a chain! He looked real mad at me and was shouting, 'Late! Late! Late!'"

Peter Lawless had apparently expanded his territory. No longer content to roam the Driskill halls or lobby, he was now stepping out into the streets to clock the city buses. (No word yet on whether he has appeared to critique the on-time status of Amtrak trains or Austin's light rail.)

Austin Ghost Tour guide Elizabeth believes she may have encountered Mr. Lawless one Halloween night. She was wrapping up a tour when a gentleman appeared at the back of the crowd, listening in. "He seemed pale; not sickly, just … colorless," she described, "as though he had on whitish make-up. It was different than Halloween costuming and make-up. He was out of place, even for that occasion. He distracted me for a moment by his expression, like I was talking about him – or someone he knew personally." Elizabeth continued by describing the odd way he had of moving through the crowd.

> *There's an acknowledgment of personal space with most adults, right? But it seemed as though this man was standing right on top of my tour guests too close for them not to see him, but they didn't appear to notice him. Even more strange was that when I tried to look for him in the crowd, I couldn't find him. Other times, I knew where he was, but only if I wasn't looking directly at him. When I finished the stories about Lawless, he vanished within the crowd. I later saw the photo from his obituary. It seemed to resemble him, but remember, I never did get a good look at him directly.*

If you try to book Peter Lawless' former room, you will be disappointed. Because there have been so many changes to the rooms and suites in the older portion of the hotel, the old room does not exist anymore. Old Austin City Directories were not specific about the room number, only listing his address as The Driskill Hotel. While his obituary mentioned his long-time residency at the hotel, the accomplishments of Peter Lawless were more important to list than his room number.

It seems ironic to me that time was of paramount importance to this railroad man. And now, all his restless spirit seems to have is time.

Col. Lawless Dies

Col. Peter J. Lawless, 80, pioneer railroad man of Austin, died in a local hospital Monday morning. He had been a resident of Austin for the past 59 years.

Chapter Seven
The Unnamed, Unknown Entities

The Grey Ghost

Much the same as Elizabeth's sighting, tour guide Alexander was telling his crowd some stories facing the large credenza in the lobby. He suddenly saw a man step out of the old bank vault; someone he described as looking "off."

> *He came around the corner and he just looked weird, like he might have had jaundice, only his pallor wasn't yellow, it was beige. The only way I can describe it was like he walked out of a black and white film or sepia photo and was milling around among the normal-looking people! I kept talking, but watched him skirt around the perimeter of the crowd, looking at me the whole time. Then he went behind a pillar and didn't come back out the other side! I paused for too long a moment, a little stunned, when a tour guest said somberly, "I saw him too. He came out of the vault." We agreed on his mode of dress as a rumpled old ill-fitting business suit and how strange his color was. I haven't gone near that bank vault since then!*

I sent Alexander the Peter Lawless obituary, but he sent word back, "Nope! It was someone different." Who? Another spirit just passing through? Maybe someone who worked at the American Bank branch that Col. Littlefield opened in the ornate Driskill lobby when he owned the hotel? The sepia-skinned stranger remains a mystery.

The Texas Ladies Man

Lead singer of the alternative rock band, "Concrete Blonde," Johnette Napolitano found both mystery and inspiration at The Driskill during a stay there in 1991. On the road opening for Sting, Johnette's tour was marked by a memorable evening. She described it as an "off-kilter sort of day" when the TV was on the fritz, she kept dropping things, and items kept falling off the bed and desk. She traveled with her cat, "Bear," who, she said, was acting strangely from the time they entered the room. Rather than bouncing off the walls or exploring the room, once she managed to get the abnormally nervous Bear out of his carrier, the cat wrapped himself into a tight furry ball in the center of the bed. Even at 3:00 a.m., after she returned from the gig and a late night hanging out with friends, Bear was in exactly the same spot as when she left the suite. "Weird cat," she thought. But things were about to get weirder for Johnette.

> *I started undressing and headed into the bathroom when I had a strong feeling someone was watching me. I walked around the suite and drew the*

curtains, although I was on the 5th floor and there was no one to see in the window. Still, I felt creepy, like someone was there. I took a bath and headed to bed. On the nightstand beside the bed was a small lamp with a pull chain, the old kind, with a silk shade. I pulled the chain, the light went out, and I turned over to sleep. The light came back on. I turned, reached over and pulled the chain. The light went out. I turned over. The light came back on. It was starting to dawn on me there was something up here. I'd been feeling creepy all day, and now I was sure someone was messing with me. I turned over and pulled the chain again, and waited in the dark. Not even a minute went by before the light came back on.

By now it was nearly 4:00 a.m. and Johnette was beginning to regret partying so late with friends in the "Live Music Capitol of the World." She reached over and pulled the cord out of the socket in the wall.

"I know you're here." she called out to the darkness."I know you won't hurt me, but I have to get to sleep! It's late and I'm tired."

As if a hand pushed it from inside, the closet door opened. The closet light, which had been left on, expanded in a single beam onto the carpet, then the bed, then Johnette, who by this time was sitting straight up in complete disbelief... naked in bed. "That was it," she exclaimed, "He was watching me take a bath, he wanted to see me and wanted the lights left on!"

She forged her sleepless night with a flirty specter into one of Concrete Blonde's more popular songs, "Ghost of A Texas Ladies Man."

"He seemed so glad to see a woman in the flesh," the lyrics admit, "And I really liked his spirit."

But who is this ghost? Like many other specters, we cannot be certain of his identity.

Annie Lennox's Wardrobe Consultant

Another singer to have a brush with the paranormal side of The Driskill is Annie Lennox, solo artist and lead singer for the "Eurhythmics." I will spare you puns of "Sweet Dreams (Are Made of This)" and launch into the tale of how Ms. Lennox was preparing for a gig in Austin. Road-weary, she laid two outfits on the bed and could not decide which one she would wear onstage that night. Thinking she might be able to make a better decision after a hot shower, she locked the door to her suite and stepped into the bathroom. Upon coming back out into her room, however, she found one dress still on the bed. The other was hung carefully in the closet. She wore the outfit left out. It obviously came highly recommended.

Animal Spirits

Although I don't know for certain which suite Annie Lennox was given, it may have been the afore-mentioned Cattle Baron Suite. If so, Annie might have had more warm and fuzzy company than she counted on!

While I was waiting for my turn on camera for a TV segment discussing the Driskill's hauntings, I overheard an interesting story told by none other than the General Manager of the hotel.

One of the few full-blown paranormal investigations conducted at The Driskill took place when the entire hotel was shut down to have the electrical system updated. (The investigation, by the way, was not done by any of the usual paranormal TV show suspects.) One of the team members who was psychically "sensitive" remarked that she felt there was a cat occupying the Cattle Baron Suite. Not knowing what else to do with a piece of information like that other than to shrug and say, "Okay. That's… interesting," the Driskill staff went about its daily business.

A few years later, though, the hotel was awarded for its "pet friendly" status by a magazine. A photo shoot was set up with docile photogenic animals making themselves at home in the hotel. But a dog handler was perplexed when his canine was set down on the carpet in the Cattle Baron Suite and the pup proceeded to race around the dining room table, barking and posturing playfully.

"I don't understand it," said the trainer. "He usually only acts that way when there's a cat around!"

The incident made me think of the scene in the movie Ghostbusters when Bill Murray's character describes conditions once ghosts are released into the world unchecked: "Human sacrifices! Cats and dogs living together! Mass hysteria!" Well, at least for the dogs.

The Playful & Helpful Spirits

Elevators seem to have a mind of their own at The Driskill. I have sometimes cautioned people waiting for the elevator to arrive, "Once you're in there, you might want to announce the floor you want and that you want the door to open when you get there. Just sayin'!" It is only because I can speak from personal experience and have heard about it happening to others.

Despite going through the normal procedures of choosing your floor and expecting to arrive there, certain elevators may take you on a little joyride, leaving you to wonder if there is some magic word that will open the door on any floor! I unintentionally crashed a wedding reception on the mezzanine after a nervous couple of minutes with other guests inside the car all expecting to be taken to the 5th floor. Oh, the elevator went to 5, but the door would not open. Then it went to 4, to the lobby, and to the mezzanine, the door remaining stubbornly closed at every floor. The car was full and the other riders squeezed in with me were no longer amused by the game. When we paused on the mezzanine with the reception's music thumping on the other side, I pleaded aloud "Fine! Mezzanine! Just open the door, please!" The elevator obeyed and we were mercifully released. As it turns out, this was a familiar story among staff members who had often been taken to floors all over the hotel, not just in the older historic portion of the hotel but the newer tower as well.

Conversely, the elevator spirits have been kind to employees, particularly those on the maintenance staff. On numerous occasions, with their arms full of boxes of supplies, struggling to push the button of the floor they want, the astonished staffer will see the floor number they want light up and the elevator swiftly takes them to their destination. When the car arrives, there is no one on that floor who could have called the elevator.

Remember Bruno, the tough guy from the security staff? He confided a story to me recently that sort of sums up the helpful nature of this spirited hotel.

> *When I first started, the guy who trained me sort of threw me into the deep end and let me fend for myself. He gave me a walky-talky and said, "Go wander around the hotel. Get yourself lost and find your way out. You'll learn more that way." So I was walking around and, yeah, I got myself good and lost! Well, they called me on the walky after a while and said, "We need you back in the office right away." And I was too proud to admit I didn't*

know where the heck I was. But then I looked down at the end of a hall and saw a ceiling light flicker. I thought, "What's that?" and went down there. When I got there, the light seemed fine. But then I looked down the next hallway, and saw a light flashing down there. I went down there, and so on, and so on, until I was led back to the office... by... something! And I thought, "Okay, this job is going to be a little different."

Welcome to my world, Bruno.

In Closing... For Now

Really, I could not title this last segment "Conclusion." That word has such finality to it; an unquestioning confidence I cannot muster with this subject matter. (Heh... "matter." Another irony.)

The Austin Ghost Tours staff will continue to collect fascinating stories and evidence at The Driskill Hotel. The spirits here epitomize the city's motto to "Keep Austin Weird." They can be original in their pranks, a sentimental lot, or sometimes mysterious and morose. They have seen exuberant life and slipped past death. We find that the essences of their personalities are still very human, only without the limitations of matter, time and space! In another setting, liberation like that might be ghostly nitroglycerine, but at this historic hotel, it makes for a never-ending paranormal party. The Driskill's guests in spirit form simply add to the hotel's long parade of colorful characters some of which are just passing through, while others would not want to be anywhere else.

The guides of Austin Ghost Tours consider it an honor to share these stories with you. We agree that it is certainly one of our favorite places to visit each week. May you feel as welcomed at The Driskill Hotel.

About the Author

Monica Ballard has been a guide and investigator with Austin Ghost Tours since 2004. She has also written episodes and assisted with production of PBS's only paranormal television show, *Haunted Texas*. She regularly blogs about her personal experiences and those of tour guests on Austin Ghost Tours' website, *www.AustinGhostTours.com*. Her experiences at The Driskill Hotel were featured on the premiere episode of Bio Channel's series, *My Ghost Story*, where the producers tried unsuccessfully to coax her into making the encounters seem much more frightening. This is Monica's third book, although she has contributed to many others. Other titles include *Star of Wonder: A Journey Back To Creativity* and *Godspeed & Happy Landings: Becoming Pilot-In-Command of Your Goals*. Both were published by Wizard Academy Press and are available through her website, *www.PerformanceMuse.com*.